Soho Theatre and On Theatre
in association with
Blind Summit present

on emotion

by Mick Gordon and Paul Broks

First performed at Soho Theatre on 5 November 2008

Soho Theatre is supported by
ACE, Bloomberg, TEQUILA\London,
Westminster City Council, The City Bridge Trust

Performances in the Lorenz Auditorium
Registered Charity No: 267234

Soho Theatre and On Theatre in association with Blind Summit present

on emotion

by Mick Gordon and Paul Broks

Cast

Lucy	**Rhian Blythe**
Anna	**Caroline Catz**
Mark	**Mark Down**
Stephen	**James Wilby**

Writer/Director	**Mick Gordon**
Writer	**Paul Broks**
Composer	**Igor Gostuski**
Designer	**Nick Barnes**
Puppetry	**Blind Summit**
Lighting Designer	**Linus Fellbom**
Sound Designer	**Mike Furness**
Assistant Director	**Athina Kasiou**
Production Manager	**Matt Noddings**
Stage Manager	**Marie Costa**
Deputy Stage Manager	**Lorna Adamson**
Wardrobe Supervisor	**Sarah Godwin**
Casting	**Nadine Hoare**
Puppet Making	**Henry Maynard**

On Theatre would like to thank:

James Hogan and Charles Glanville for their continuing support. Without them this production would not have been possible.

The British Council and in particular: Ivana Djurisic, British Council Belgrade and Andrew Jones, British Council London.

RHIAN BLYTHE LUCY

After training at Queen Margaret University College in Edinburgh, Rhian returned to Wales where she became a resident actor with The National Theatre of Wales for two years, playing many parts including Juliet in Shakespeare's **Romeo and Juliet**. Since then she has worked vastly in Welsh theatre and television. Earlier this year Rhian performed at the Brits off Broadway festival, New York in **Blink**, a new play by Ian Rowlands. In August of this year she won The Stage Award for Best Actress at the Edinburgh Fringe Festival for her portrayal of Jonesy in Mick Gordon's production of **Deep Cut**.

CAROLINE CATZ ANNA

Caroline trained at RADA. Theatre includes **Shopping and Fucking** (West End/world tour), **Six Degrees Of Separation** (Royal Court/West End), **Dogs Barking** (The Bush Theatre), **If We Are Women** (Greenwich/ Richmond) and **The Recruiting Officer** (Chichester Festival). Television credits include Louisa Glasson in **Doc Martin, Murder In Suburbia** (two series), Cheryl Hutchins in **The Vice** (five series), **In Denial Of Murder, Real Men, All Quiet On The Preston Front**, Rosie Fox in **The Bill** and **Hotel Babylon, The Guilty** and **Stolen Child**. Film credits include **Look Me In The Eye** and Michael Winterbottom's **Under The Sun**.

MARK DOWN MARK

Mark is an actor, a doctor and artistic director of Blind Summit Theatre which he founded in 1997 with Nick Barnes. For Blind Summit he has written, directed and performed in **Tramping the Boards**, **Mr China's Son**, **Martin's Wedding**, **Pirate Puppetry**, **Low Life**, **Madam Butterfly** at the ENO, Lithuania National Opera and Metropolitan Opera in New York, **Real Man** and **An Odde Angel**. He was director of puppetry on **Faeries** at ROH2, **Shunkin** by Complicite, **Black River Falls** for Bob Karper, **The Time Step** with Linda Marlowe, **Cherevichki** at Garsington Opera, **Killing Time**, **A Puppet in the Works** for Young People's Theatre at BAC, **A Dulditch Angel** for Eastern Angles and **Falstaff** for Stanley Hall Opera. He is a visiting lecturer at Central School of Speech and Drama and East 15. He still occasionally performs **The Spaceman** on tour and played a small role (Adam) in **EastEnders**.

JAMES WILBY STEPHEN

Theatre includes **Don Juan** (Lyric, Hammersmith); **Helping Harry** (Jermyn Street Theatre); **A Patriot For Me** (RSC); **The Common Pursuit** (Phoenix); **The Tempest**, **Salonika**, **Jane Eyre** (Chichester Festival Theatre); **As You Like It** (Manchester Royal Exchange); **Chips With Everything** (Leeds Playhouse); **Who's Afraid Of Virginia Woolf** (Belgrade Theatre) and **Another Country** (Queen's Theatre).
Television includes **A Risk Worth Taking**, **Clapham Junction**, **Futureshock: Comet**, **The Last Days Of The Raj**, **Lewis**, **Little Devil**, **Miss Marple**, **Jericho**, **Foyle's War**, **Silent Witness**, **Island At War**, **Sparkling Cyanide**, **Murder In Mind**, **Bertie And Elizabeth**, **Nothing But The Truth**, **Trial And Retribution IV**, **The Woman In White**, **The Dark Room**, **Treasure Seekers**, **Witness Against Hitler**, **Crocodile Shoes**, **You Me And It**, **Lady Chatterley**, **Adam Bede**, **Tell Me That You Love Me**, **Mother Love**, **A Tale Of Two Cities**, **Storyteller** and **Dutch Girls**.
Film includes **Shadows In The Sun**, **Lady Godiva**, **Gravida**, **Just One Of Those Things**, **Gosford Park**, **Jump Tomorrow**, **Cotton Mary**, **Tom's Midnight Garden**, **Regeneration**, **Un Partie d'echec**, **Howard's End**, **Immaculate Conception**, **A Handful Of Dust** and **Maurice**.

MICK GORDON WRITER/DIRECTOR

Mick Gordon is Artistic Director of On Theatre and On Film and is Head of MA/MFA Directing at East 15 and Senior Researcher, Theatre and Mind Unit, Plymouth University. He was Trevor Nunn's Associate Director at the Royal National Theatre and was Director of the National's Transformation Season. Previously he was Artistic Director of London's Gate Theatre.
For On Theatre: **On Emotion** with Paul Broks, **On Religion** with A C Grayling, **On Ego** with Paul Broks, Soho Theatre London; **On Love** in

Uzbekistan, Ilhom Theatre Tashkent; **On Love, On Death** with Marie de Hennezel, Gate Theatre London.

Other theatre includes: **Deep Cut** (Sherman Theatre Cardiff, Traverse Theatre Edinburgh); **Grimms Tales** (Dusko Radovic Belgrade); **Dancing at Lughnasa** (Lyric Theatre Belfast); **Optic Trilogy, A Play in Swedish** (English and Italian Dramatan Theatre Stockholm); **War, Lovers, The Real Thing, Betrayal** (Strindberg Theatre Stockholm); **A Prayer for Owen Meany, The Walls, Le Pub!** (National Theatre London); **Monkey!** (Young Vic Theatre London); **Trust** (Royal Court Theatre London); **Salome** (Riverside Studios London); **Godspell** (Chichester Festival Theatre); **My Fair Lady, Closer, Art** (National Theatre Buenos Aires); **Volunteers, Marathon, Une Tempête** (Gate Theatre London); **Measure for Measure** (English Touring Theatre).

PAUL BROKS WRITER

Paul is a neuropsychologist based at Plymouth University. He gained recognition as a writer with **Into The Silent Land** (Atlantic Books, 2003) which mixes neurological case stories, fiction and memoir. It was shortlisted for the Guardian First Book Award and has been translated into 12 languages to date. Paul is a regular contributor to Prospect magazine and writes a monthly column for The Times. Since co-writing **On Ego** with Mick Gordon he has worked with filmmaker Ian Knox on **Martino Unstrung** (Sixteen Films, 2008) a documentary feature about legendary jazz guitarist Pat Martino, described by **All About Jazz** as 'Perhaps the finest documentary about a jazz musician ever made'. Paul's next book, **The Laws Of Magic**, is forthcoming from Atlantic Books.

IGOR GOSTUSKI COMPOSER

Igor was born in Belgrade in 1966 and studied composition at Belgrade Music Academy. At the end of the eighties, he formed an artistic project called Magnificent 7, with six other associate composers. The idea was to bring contemporary art music closer to the audience by combining genres and media. Gostuski's Toccatta for piano was one of the first music videos of its kind produced by TV Belgrade in former Yugoslavia. This video was also presented at the tenth fringe film and video festival in Edinburgh. He has composed stage music since 1990, writing for classical and contemporary pieces, non-verbal theatre and modern dance performances. Recent work includes Molière's **The Learned Ladies** (National Theatre of Belgrade); Howard Barker's **Minna** (Theatre M.b.h Vienna); Fernando Arabal's **Carta da amor**, Marija Stojanovic's **Tesla – Total Reflection** (International Theater Festival 'BITEF') and Lucas Svensson's **Klaus and Erika** (Malo Pozoriste Dusko Radovic). Gostuski has collaborated with leading directors and theatres in Serbia including

Yougoslav Drama Theatre, Belgrade Drama Theatre, Atelje 212 and Malo Pozoriste Dusko Radovic.

NICK BARNES DESIGNER

Nick Barnes is co-artistic director of Blind Summit Theatre which he founded in 1997 with Mark Down. Nick designs, makes puppets and performs for Blind Summit. He studied drama at Hull University and Theatre Design at the Slade School of Fine Art. He trained in puppetry with Philippe Genty at the International Institute of the Marionette (France). He has designed operas and musicals at home and abroad including **West Side Story** and **Showboat** (Austria); **Martin Guerre** (Denmark); **20,000 Leagues Under the Sea** (Theatre Royal Stratford East); **Miss Saigon** (Gothenburg Opera) and **Hansel and Gretel** (Norwegian National Opera). He has incorporated puppets into many of his designs.

BLIND SUMMIT PUPPETRY

Blind Summit Theatre was founded in 1997 by Nick Barnes and Mark Down. Company productions include: **Tramping the Boards** (2001); **Mr China's Son** (2002); **The Spaceman** (2003); **Martin's Wedding** (2004); **Pirate Puppetry** (2004); **A Puppet in the Works** (2004); **Low Life** (2005); **Real Man** (2007); **An Odde Angel** (2008). Puppetry design and direction credits include **Cherevichki** (Garsington Opera 2004); **A Dulditch Angel** (Eastern Angles, 2005); **Madam Butterfly** (ENO 2005, LNOBT 2006, Met Opera 2006, 2007, 2008); **Ramayana** (Lyric Hammersmith, West Yorkshire Playhouse, Bristol Old Vic 2007); **The Time Step** (Linda Marlowe 2008); **Shunkin** (Complicite at Setagaya Theatre 2008); **Black River Falls** (Bob Karper 2008) and **Faeries** (ROH2, The Egg Bath 2008).

LINUS FELLBOM LIGHTING DESIGNER

Since his debut as a lighting designer in 1995, Linus has designed over 130 productions. He has worked at most of the bigger venues around Sweden and has also been engaged at theatres and opera houses in cities like Oldenburg, Berlin, Innsbruck, Riga, Lodz, Warsaw, Cape Town, London, Oslo and Copenhagen. In 2005 Linus made his debut as a stage director with **Sympathy for the Devil** by Lucas Svensson at Strindberg's Intimate Theatre in Stockholm. In 2006 he directed Shakespeare's **Richard III** for Riksteatern in Sweden and in 2008 he directed Carl Maria von Weber's opera **Der Freischütz** for the Swedish Folkopera in Stockholm. Linus designed the lighting for **On Ego** in 2005 and **On Religion** in 2006, both directed by Mick Gordon at Soho Theatre.

MIKE FURNESS SOUND DESIGNER

Theatre sound designs in 2007/8 include **Sweet Cider** (Arcola); **Deep Cut** (Sherman/Traverse); **The Changeling** (ETT/Nottingham Playhouse); Lyrical M.C. (Tamasha) **Fantastic Mr Fox** (Open Air Theatre Regents Park); **A Fine Balance** (Hampstead Theatre); **Child Of The Divide** (Tamasha US Tour); **Someone Else's Shoes** (Soho Theatre). Other productions include **All's Well That Ends Well, As You Like It** (RSC); **Mother Courage** (National Theatre); **Blues In The Night, The Witches, Ladyday, The BFG** (West End); **The Trouble With Asian Men** (Tamasha); **On Religion** (On Theatre/Soho Theatre); **The Manchurian Candidate** (Lyric Hammersmith) and productions for The Tricycle, Paines Plough, Bristol Old Vic, Birmingham Rep, West Yorkshire Playhouse and Edinburgh, Brighton and Salisbury Festivals. He also produces talking books and designs sound systems for a broad range of live events worldwide.

ATHINA KASIOU ASSISTANT DIRECTOR

Athina's directing credits include **Karagiozes Exposed** (Arcola Theatre, Divaldo Na Pradle Prague, Experimental Stage of National Theatre of Cyprus); **Mr Marmalade** (stage reading, Finborough Theatre); **Tasting Apples/ Who Stole Mee?** (Canal Café Theatre); **Laba Laba** (ISI, Bali) **Play** by Beckett (Mdx, London) and **Action** by Shepard (Semel Theatre, Boston). Assistant Director credits include **Gianni Schicchi** and **Yolanta** (Royal Academy of Music); **Private Jokes, Public Places** (New End Theatre); **Hamlet, the Outsider** (Southwark Playhouse); **Our Lady Of 121st Street** (Speakeasy). Athina holds an MFA in Theatre Directing from Middlesex University and a BA from Emerson College, with further training at GITIS Academy of Dramatic Arts Moscow, ISI Indonesian Art Institute in Bali. In 2008 she was part of the Lincoln Center Director's Lab (New York). She is the founder of Open Arts theatre (www.openartstheatre.com). She is currently collaborating with visual artist Carl Krull on a new project entitled **In Two Minds**.

On Theatre

Each piece of our work is on a given subject: Death, Love, Ego, Religion, Emotion. We call our work theatre essays. The starting point is always a question. And each piece is an attempt to explore its subject with intellectual rigour and theatrical aplomb. On Theatre's work is made in the UK, and supported by Arts Council England. We work with international artists and theatres and when we do our work is supported by the British Council. On Theatre's work has been seen in the UK, North America, Europe, Australia and Uzbekistan.

Artistic Director and Producer: **Mick Gordon**
Associate Director: **Chris Haydon**

Board Of Directors:
Gavin Irwin (Chair)
Adam Glass
Joe Smith
Tara Hull
Nina Steiger

Patrons:
Peter Brook
Trevor Nunn

PERFORMANCE PROVOCATIVE AND COMPELLING THEATRE, COMEDY AND CABARET **TALKS** VIBRANT DEBATES ON CULTURE, THE ARTS AND THE WAY WE LIVE **SOHO CONNECT** A THRIVING EDUCATION, COMMUNITY AND OUTREACH PROGRAMME **WRITERS' CENTRE** DISCOVERING AND NURTURING NEW WRITERS AND ARTISTS **SOHO THEATRE BAR** SERVING TASTY, AFFORDABLE FOOD AND DRINK FROM 12PM TILL LATE.

'The capital's centre for daring international drama.'
EVENING STANDARD

'A jewel in the West End.'
BBC LONDON

THE TERRACE BAR
Drinks can be taken into the auditorium and are available from the Terrace Bar on the second floor.

SOHO THEATRE ONLINE
Giving you the latest information and previews of upcoming shows, Soho Theatre can be found on facebook, myspace and youtube as well as at sohotheatre.com

EMAIL INFORMATION LIST
For regular programme updates and offers visit sohotheatre.com/mailing

HIRING THE THEATRE
Soho Theatre has a range of rooms and spaces for hire. Please contact the theatre on 020 7287 5060 or go to sohotheatre.com/hires for further details.

THE SOHO THEATRE DEVELOPMENT CAMPAIGN

Soho Theatre receives core funding from Arts Council England, London. In order to provide as diverse a programme as possible and expand our audience development and outreach work, we rely upon additional support from trusts, foundations, individuals and businesses. All of our major sponsors share a common commitment to developing new areas of activity and encouraging creative partnerships between business and the arts. We are immensely grateful for the invaluable support from our sponsors and donors and wish to thank them for their continued commitment.

Soho Theatre has a Friends Scheme in support of its education programme and work developing new writers and reaching new audiences.

To find out how to become a Friend of Soho Theatre, contact the development department on **020 7478 0143**, or visit **sohotheatre.com**.

SOHO STAFF

Artistic Director:
Lisa Goldman
Executive Director:
Mark Godfrey (sabbatical)
Acting Executive Director:
Catherine Thornborrow

BOARD OF DIRECTORS
Nicholas Allott (chair)
Sue Robertson (vice chair)
David Aukin
Norma Heyman
Jeremy King
Neil Mendoza
Simon Minty
Michael Naughton
David Pelham
Roger Wingate
Christopher Yu

HONORARY PATRONS
Bob Hoskins (President)
Peter Brook CBE
Simon Callow
Gurinder Chadha
Sir Richard Eyre CBE

ARTISTIC TEAM
Writers' Centre Director:
Nina Steiger (sabbatical)
Soho Connect Director:
Suzanne Gorman
Casting Director: **Nadine Hoare**
Producer – Late Night Programme:
Steve Lock
Writers' Centre Assistant:
Sheena Bucktowonsing
International Associate: **Paul Sirett**
Artistic Associate: **Esther Richardson**
Director of Talks: **Palash Davé**
Soho Connect Workshop Leader:
Don McCamphill
Senior Reader: **Dale Heinan**

ADMINISTRATION
Acting General Manager:
Erin Gavaghan
Financial Controller: **Kevin Dunn**
Finance Officer: **Kate Wickens**

MARKETING, DEVELOPMENT
AND PRESS
Marketing Director: **Jacqui Gellman**
Acting Head of Development: **Zoe Crick**
Marketing Manager: **Nicki Marsh**
Press and Public Relations: **Nancy Poole** (020 7478 0142)
Development Assistant:
Zebina Nelson-Myrie
Marketing and New Media Assistant:
Alex Fleming
Access Officer: **Charlie Swinbourne**

BOX OFFICE AND FRONT OF HOUSE
Front of House and Events Manager:
Jennifer Dromey
Box Office Manager:
Charlotte Edmundson
Box Office Assistants:
Danielle Baker, Lou Beere, Philip Elvy, Tamsin Flessey, Lynne Forbes, Louise Green, Eniola Jaiyeoba, Helen Matthews, Leah Read, Becca Savory, Traci Leigh Scarlett, Nida Vohra, Tom Webb and **Natalie Worrall**.
Duty Managers: **Colin Goodwin, Martin Murphy**.
Front of House staff: **Carla Almeida, Beth Aynsley, Thylda Bares, Adrian Fubara, Louise Hall, Obi Iwumene, Kyle Jenkins, Bea Kempton, Tony Dinh Le, Matthew Lewis, Mutana Mohmed, James Munroe, Kate Mulley, Monique Sterling** and **Gemma Strong**.

PRODUCTION
Production Manager: **Matt Noddings**
Technical Manager: **Nick Blount**
Head of Lighting: **Christoph Wagner**
Technician: **Natalie Smith**

21 Dean Street,
London W1D 3NE
sohotheatre.com
Admin: 020 7287 5060
Box Office: 020 7478 0100

Individuality matters to our partnership.

GOODMAN DERRICK LLP is delighted to be Soho Theatre's sole supporting partner.

We do not seek to dramatise. As a firm with a broad legal practice, we want to meet your legal needs by understanding your business and by developing a close working relationship with you.

Our performance aims to reduce the burden of the legal aspects of decision making, enabling you to make the most of opportunities whilst limiting your business, financial and legal risks.

We structure our services with a view to saving expensive management time, thereby producing cost-effective decision making.

We take pride in watching our clients' businesses prosper and assisting them in that process wherever we can.

For more information about how we can help you or your business visit www.gdlaw.co.uk or contact Belinda Copland bcopland@gdlaw.co.uk tel: +44 (0)20 7404 0606

GOODMAN DERRICK LLP

ALMEIDA
THEATRE

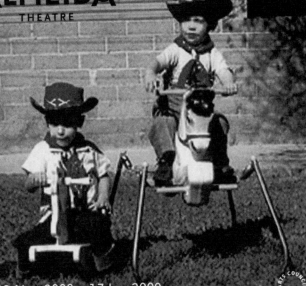

20 Nov 2008 – 17 Jan 2009
European Premiere

In a Dark Dark House
By Neil LaBute

Cast: Steven Mackintosh,
David Morrissey and Kira Sternbach

Director Michael Attenborough
Design Lez Brotherston
Lighting Howard Harrison
Sound Howard Wood

Tickets £6 – £29.50

Box Office **020 7359 4404**
Book and join e-list at **www.almeida.co.uk**

Principal Sponsor: Coutts & Co

Main photo Crafty Walt, David Morrissey photograph Lorenzo Agius/Getty Image. Almeida Theatre registered charity no 282167

ON EMOTION

First published in 2008 by Oberon Books Ltd
521 Caledonian Road, London N7 9RH
Tel: 020 7607 3637 / Fax: 020 7607 3629
e-mail: info@oberonbooks.com
www.oberonbooks.com

A catalogue record for this book is available from the British
Library.

Cover image by Mark Goddard

ISBN: 978-1-84002-883-6

Printed in Great Britain by CPI Antony Rowe, Chippenham

theatre *n.* 1 A building designed for the performance of plays, operas, etc. 2 The writing or production of plays. 3 A setting for dramatic or important events. [From Latin *theatrum*, from Greek *theatron*, place for viewing.]

essay *n.* 1 A short literary composition dealing with a subject analytically or speculatively. 2 To attempt or endeavour; effort. 3 To test or try out. [From Old French *essaier*, to attempt.]

Contents

Are we just the puppets of our emotions?

In our previous Theatre Essay, *On Ego*, the neurologist Paul Broks and I examined brain architecture in relation to personal identity. Now, in *On Emotion*, we begin to deconstruct the architecture of the theatre's most vital tool: emotion.

It is generally agreed that there are six basic emotions: fear, sadness, anger, surprise, joy and disgust. We share these basic emotions with the great apes and other mammals. And yet they are central to our human experience. They make us what we are. They give our lives meaning; make life worth living, or perhaps ending. They raise us to the pinnacle of spiritual and artistic experience. They do all of this. And yet, they often seem to be beyond our control.

As with a written essay the starting point for a Theatre Essay is a question. And finding the most theatrically vibrant question to ask of our theme informs the making of our work. Investigating emotion's relationship to thought would be fundamental. So we started with: *Are we pulled and pushed by forces we can't control?* Moved to: *Is rational thought like so much steam from a kettle, secondary to the heat?* Got lost in: *Are we simply the dupes of nature's cruel joke: the illusion of free will?* And finally arrived at: *Are we just the puppets of our emotions?*

The use of puppets and puppetry to explore the human condition has a noble history. Puppetry pre-dates theatre, and has been used in almost all human societies both as an entertainment and ceremonially. It seems that the mechanistic nature of puppetry allows us a space to think about our own workings. And the magic of puppetry, the transformation of an inanimate object into something living, raises questions about the magical thinking that connects us all.

To take responsibility for our emotions seems crucial if we want to build successful relationships with ourselves and with others. How to do this, and remain open to the new experiences that life brings, is one of the great challenges and joys of being human.

Mick Gordon

Characters

STEPHEN
A Cognitive Behavioural Therapist. Late fifties.

LUCY
Stephen's daughter. A young actress.

ANNA
Lucy's friend. A puppet maker.

MARK
Stephen's son. A young man at a slight angle to
the universe.

Note: The printed text may vary slightly from the text as performed.

Pre-Set

Surrounding the playing area, on the walls perhaps, the stars of the Northern Hemisphere. A sofa in the middle of the stage. Sitting on it, a Bunraku style puppet, three feet tall perhaps, of MARK in a silver space suit. The puppet has his hand on his space helmet, which sits beside him. He is clearly pre-mission. To the side, two modern chairs and a small table appropriate for STEPHEN's therapy room, a sculpting easel for ANNA's studio, her digital camera on a tripod and a telescope on a stand.

Music.

Slowly to black during which the puppet disappears behind the sofa. The music builds to:

Scene 1

Out of time. ANNA and LUCY.

LUCY looks at ANNA. LUCY laughs.

LUCY: Are you fucking my Dad?

Beat.

Are you fucking my Dad?

Beat.

Answer the question Anna.

ANNA: Lucy!

LUCY: You wouldn't. How could you? You would never. You're my best friend.

ANNA: Yes, I am.

LUCY: I saved your fucking life you fucked up slut!

ANNA: Can you hear what you're saying, Lucy?

LUCY: Do you suck his cock?

ANNA: Stop this. Right now.

LUCY: Do you suck my father's cock? Don't answer that. Well
do you? Answer my fucking question, at least do me the
courtesy of answering my fucking question. You whore.
You disgusting fucking total whore.

ANNA: I think you'd better go.

LUCY: You think I'd better go?

ANNA: It think it would be sensible.

LUCY: You think it would be *sensible?* You're fucking my father.
And you think it would be *sensible* if I go?

ANNA: What's happened to you?

LUCY: Nothing's *happened.*

ANNA: Something's happened, to make you this frightened.

LUCY: I'm not *frightened.*

ANNA: You're frightened Lucy. It's why you sleep with so
many stupid men and think it's the same as falling in love.

Beat.

LUCY: I should have let you kill yourself.

ANNA: Maybe you should.

LUCY: You really are fucking mad!

ANNA: And you are a small, frightened, pathetic, little child.

LUCY: Well at least I'm not a *baby-killer!*

*Music. ANNA attacks LUCY. LUCY tries to escape but ANNA has her.
Now fighting: hair pulling, messy, dirty, violent. Now they fight in
slow motion. During this, and still in slow motion, ANNA throws
a glass at LUCY. At this point, STEPHEN and MARK enter. In slow*

motion, STEPHEN puppets the glass from ANNA's hand towards LUCY's head.

STEPHEN: Mr Spock.

MARK: Yes Captain.

STEPHEN: The women on your planet are logical.

MARK: Yes Captain.

STEPHEN: That's the only planet in the galaxy that can make that claim.

LUCY ducks, STEPHEN puppets the glass over LUCY's head. MARK catches it. As soon as he does, the two men come out of slow motion, moving normally. The two women remain in slow motion, grabbing the back cushions from the sofa to hit each other with. As they do, STEPHEN observes them.

STEPHEN: Does your logic find this fascinating, Mr Spock?

MARK: Fascinating is a word I use for the unexpected. In this case, I should think interesting would suffice.

STEPHEN: You'd make a splendid computer, Mr Spock.

MARK: Thank you Captain.

In slow motion, LUCY throws her cushion at ANNA. STEPHEN puppets it in slow motion. It hits ANNA, knocking her to the ground. MARK is now behind ANNA helping her to fall in slow motion. Now, the sound of a space rocket blasting off. Smoke and light begin to come out of the sofa. MARK moves behind the sofa and in slow motion opens the two remaining bottom cushions, like two enormous space-age dock doors. Then he disappears behind the sofa to take the head of the puppet. LUCY operates the feet, ANNA the right hand, STEPHEN operates a smoke machine in front of the sofa. Suddenly the opening theme music from Star Trek *begins. During this, the space-man puppet rises from behind the sofa and through the smoke. The puppet space-walks over the sofa, as if in zero gravity, then he stands to tell us.*

MARK: (*Mimics.*) 'These are the voyages of the star ship,
Enterprise. Its five year mission: to explore strange new
worlds... To seek out new life and new civilisations...
To boldly go where no man has gone before...'

*The puppet blasts off into space. A choreographed sequence as
STEPHEN comes forward down stage right. The puppet flies in slow
motion towards STEPHEN and uses him to kick off into space.*

Music changes.

STEPHEN: Are we just the puppets of our emotions? Pulled
and pushed by forces we can't control? Automata? Dupes
of nature's cruel joke: the illusion of free will? Is rational
thought like so much steam from a kettle? Secondary to the
heat?

*STEPHEN looks at the puppet, which is now centre stage and spinning
in mid-air in the foetal position.*

No. (*To audience.*) No. Take charge of the head and the heart
will follow. We're free to choose. But we must *choose* to be
free to choose.

*The puppet slowly falls to the ground in a prayer position as we hear
(recorded) a girl's voice reciting an eerie little prayer. STEPHEN fetches
one of his chairs and sits down to listen. ANNA stops puppeting first,
placing the puppet's right hand gently to its side.*

CHILD: Now I lay me down to sleep,
I pray the Lord my soul to keep.
If I should die before I wake,
I pray the Lord my soul to take.

ANNA: It won't stop.

STEPHEN: What is that?

ANNA: It's...it's a...

LUCY: It sounds like a prayer.

ANNA: It's a prayer.

MARK and LUCY float the puppet, still in prayer position, gently up stage.

LUCY: Where did you hear it?

MARK: Anna.

LUCY: Anna?

MARK: She said it to Dad.

LUCY: Have you been in Dad's room again Mark?

MARK: My feet went in, so I had to go too.

LUCY: Mark. You know the rule.

MARK: Dad's room is private.

LUCY: Dad's room is private.

ANNA: Now I lay me down to sleep.
I pray the Lord my soul to keep.

MARK: I like puppets more than prayers.

ANNA: I can't make it stop. And I have to. I have to make them stop.

STEPHEN: Okay. I think we need to go back to the beginning.

Music. Lights change. MARK and LUCY exit.

Scene 2

STEPHEN's room. Down stage two therapy chairs. Mid-stage the sofa. Up stage a large projection screen, unacknowledged by either STEPHEN or ANNA.

STEPHEN: Fear.

Sound and on one-sixth of the Screen: ANNA's face: FEAR.

What is it that you fear?

ANNA: Thoughts.

STEPHEN: Thoughts?

ANNA: My thoughts.

ANNA looks at STEPHEN.

They won't let me sleep.

Sound and on one-sixth of the Screen: ANNA's face: SADNESS.

STEPHEN: And the sadness?

ANNA: No. Yes. No. Not sadness.

STEPHEN: What else frightens you?

ANNA: Ghosts.

STEPHEN: You believe in ghosts?

ANNA: No.

STEPHEN: I see.

ANNA: And going mad.

STEPHEN: Yes.

ANNA: Am I going mad?

STEPHEN: No.

ANNA: Then why am I so scared of the dark?

Lights dim, except on STEPHEN and ANNA, as we hear.

CHILD: If I should die before I wake,
  I pray the Lord my soul to take.

STEPHEN: Fears follow us from childhood,

ANNA: But I'm not a child Stephen. I'm thirty-four.

STEPHEN: The prayer?

ANNA: When the lights go out. It rises from the dark, and then
  her face.

STEPHEN: Her face?

Sound and on one-sixth of the Screen: ANNA's face: SURPRISE.

ANNA: (*Laughing.*) It shouldn't surprise me. It shouldn't
  shock me. It doesn't. Why does it always *shock* me? Still.
  Still… And then…then I think, thoughts, in my brain, the
  thoughts, in my head, and I can't, but I know, I do, I know
  there's only one thing I can… I feel sick. Oh shit. God, I
  think I'm going to be sick…

ANNA retches.

Sound and on one-sixth of the Screen: ANNA's face: DISGUST.

STEPHEN: We are born to be afraid. Fear is the most
  fundamental, the oldest of our emotions. We need it
  to survive. But fear can consume us. It's a question of
  understanding the mechanism. Once we understand the
  mechanisms of fear we can begin to bring it under control.
  We don't have to be the puppet of our emotions.

ANNA: Fuck you! FUCK YOU!

Sound and on one-sixth of the Screen: ANNA's face: ANGER.

  Sorry. No. I didn't mean that. I didn't. I didn't mean to say
  that. I'm not in control Stephen. They're out of control. I'm
  just so tired. I'm just so *angry.* Why am I so fucking *angry*?

Sound and on Screen: A light flashes where the sixth face should appear then black.

STEPHEN: Intrusive thoughts. They overwhelm…

A heart-beat begins to slowly build.

ANNA: They grip. Cold fingers at my shoulder. And…

Sounds.

I hear things. Water dripping in the pipes. The fridge humming in the kitchen, scratching sounds, creaks, my heart beating, thump-thumping into the pillow. And I know it's only a pump, a mechanical thing, and like all the other sounds, if it stopped it would be quiet. I want it to be quiet.

STEPHEN: Intrusive, catastrophic thoughts.

ANNA: And ghosts. What about the ghosts?

STEPHEN: Classic vicious circle: Thoughts, symptoms – pounding heart – further anxious thoughts, intensified symptoms, intensified thoughts, and a great catastrophic misinterpretation at the centre of the vortex…

ANNA: I want to die.

STEPHEN: No you don't. You're here.

ANNA: You don't know. You say you do but you don't. No one knows! No one.

Sounds stop.

STEPHEN: It's a question of breaking the circle Anna.

Sound. Black out except for the five faces then another sound and a light flashes to reveal:

Scene 3

ANNA's studio. A puppet-maker's equipment. On the floor, a puppet of, and for, MARK. It is the spaceman. This time slightly unfinished. The blank head of a puppet she is working on, on a sculpting easel. Downstage, a camera on a tripod. ANNA is making faces into the camera. The same faces from the previous scene which are still present on the screen up stage. The face she is trying to make, joy, is clearly causing her problems. LUCY enters and stands observing, holding her bag, inside her script of Shakespeare's As You Like It.

ANNA: Bollocks!

LUCY: No it's good.

ANNA: It's supposed to be *joy*.

LUCY: Oh.

They look at the frozen portraits. Doesn't look much like joy.

Well it's…em…

ANNA: …not very fucking *joyful* is what it is.

LUCY: Do you want me to do it? I'm very good at joy.

ANNA: It's for a self-portrait Lucy.

LUCY: Oh. (*Laughs at the irony…*) Well, the others are good.

ANNA: Yeah.

LUCY: You're making a puppet of *yourself*?

ANNA: What are you doing here? It's not four o'clock yet.

LUCY: Need some help.

ANNA: Is Mark with you?

LUCY: Outside.

ANNA: Oh Lucy. What about his routine?

LUCY: He's fine. He's got his binoculars. Please Anna.

ANNA: He's going to get upset.

LUCY: Please. Just ten minutes.

ANNA: (*Giving in.*) Ugh!

LUCY: Love you! Scene Three.

LUCY hands ANNA her script. Her lines are highlighted.

LUCY: Mine are the…

ANNA: Highlighted ones. Yes I know… 'Why cousin, why Rosalind! Cupid have mercy, not a word?'

LUCY: 'Not one to throw at a dog.'

ANNA: 'No thy words are too precious to be cast away upon curs.'

LUCY: Slow down.

ANNA: 'Throw some of them at me; lame me with reasons.'

LUCY: 'Then there were two…' I don't get that.

ANNA: Your stupidity is wilful.

LUCY: I don't have to know what it means I just have to sound like I do.

ANNA: How can you be so successful?

LUCY: I'm very malleable.

ANNA: Who told you that?

LUCY: No one.

ANNA: No one.

LUCY: No.

ANNA: What does malleable mean?

LUCY: (*Definite.*) Pretty.

ANNA: How can I be friends with you?

LUCY: Maybe you're a lesbian.

ANNA: (*Can't help but smile.*) Fuck off.

LUCY: She smiles! There you go, the beginnings of joy!

ANNA: I can't believe this is my life.

LUCY: 'Then there were two cousins laid up, when the one should be lamed with reasons and the other should be mad without any.' Mad without any?

ANNA: Resign now.

LUCY: Stop it. Mad without what?

ANNA: Reason.

LUCY: Without reason?

ANNA: Without reason we would all be mad.

LUCY: Oh I see. Oh shit. (*LUCY laughs.*) Sorry Anna, I didn't mean, it's not…

ANNA: I'm not *mad* Lucy.

LUCY: No. I know but…

ANNA: I'm not mad.

LUCY: Sorry. '…when the one should be lamed with reasons and the other should be mad without any.'

LUCY is about to step over an unfinished puppet.

ANNA: Don't step over him!

LUCY bends down to pick up the puppet.

LUCY: Oh! (*Laughing.*) Is this Mark's?

ANNA: Can you just leave him alone please. He's not finished.

LUCY: Look at his little suit! I loved your classes. Focus. Fixed point. Breathing.

ANNA: Can you just please. Just put him down.

LUCY: Breathing is the key!

LUCY uses the puppet in a cavalier way.

ANNA: Lucy!

LUCY: Okay. Fuck's sake.

LUCY stops. She has pushed ANNA too far. LUCY puts the puppet down on a chair.

ANNA goes back to the lines.

ANNA: 'But is all this for your father?'

LUCY: 'No, some of it is for my child's father.' How was the old man?

ANNA: Em… He was… Lovely actually.

LUCY: Good.

ANNA: No, really. You were right. He's brilliant. You know. Helpful.

LUCY: Told you.

ANNA: And not so old.

LUCY: That man spends more on skin care than I do!

ANNA: Impossible.

LUCY laughs.

LUCY: It's where I get it from. My *vanity*. I get my *vanity* from my father!

ANNA: What's going on? Why are you so giddy today? What's happened?

LUCY: (*Laughing.*) I'm not *giddy*!

ANNA: Yes you are. Look at you. You're totally giddy.

LUCY: I am not giddy! Continue with the lines please. Something about 'burs'.

ANNA: 'Burs… petticoats will catch them.'

LUCY: 'I could shake them off my coat, these burs are in my heart.' (*Laughs.*)

ANNA: What is it?

LUCY: I'm acting!

ANNA: Oh. I see. Very good.

LUCY: Act to feel Anna. Make yourself laugh and joy will follow!

ANNA: 'Hem them away.'

LUCY: 'I would try if I could cry hem and have him.' He's called Brian!

ANNA: I knew it!

LUCY: Brian!

ANNA: Not the cameraman?

LUCY: (*Correction.*) Cinematographer.

ANNA: I thought he was old enough to be your, you know.

LUCY: He is!

ANNA: Brian?

LUCY: I know!

ANNA: Brian the cameraman?

LUCY: (*Correction.*) Cinematographer. I could feel him watching me.

ANNA: Isn't that his job?

LUCY: No! Really watching me. Intensely. And I knew he was watching me intensely. You know when you just know when someone's watching you intensely?

ANNA: *Intense Brian.*

LUCY: Stop saying it.

ANNA: You didn't?

LUCY: (*Very serious.*) Of course I didn't.

ANNA: Good.

LUCY: Of course I did! (*Laughs.*)

ANNA: Oh Lucy.

LUCY: I know! What a *slut!*

LUCY spreads her legs dramatically and whoops.

ANNA: Remember what happened the last time…

LUCY: This is totally different!

ANNA looks at LUCY: You always say that.

It is!

ANNA: Well, I hope you've at least thought about…

LUCY: (*Mocking.*) …about the consequences of my actions. Of course I have. So now I'm playing hard to get. Treat 'em mean, keep 'em keen and all that. He's left about a million messages! Be happy for me Anna! And for God's sake don't tell my Dad, he's got enough on his plate.

ANNA: What do you mean don't tell your Dad?

LUCY: I mean don't tell my Dad. I know what therapy's like. Things just… you know, slip out.

ANNA: Oh Lucy.

LUCY: And I'm not introducing you until you can do joy.

ANNA: Whatever.

LUCY: You're going to love him!

Down stage, a pair of binoculars enters, leading a naked MARK. The binoculars are clearly looking for something. They see ANNA's camera and recognise a friend.

ANNA: Hello Mark.

The binoculars look at ANNA. People are strange.

MARK: (*To the room. Perfect mimic.*) Please replace the hand-set and try again.

The binoculars now see what they were looking for, the puppet.

LUCY: No Mark. It's not finished.

The binoculars scan the puppet.

MARK: My face. In space. In Space. Dun Dun Da! The final frontier.

The binoculars have now become the star ship Enterprise.

'These are the voyages of the star ship Enterprise…'

LUCY: Now it's *Star Trek.* He loves Mr Spock.

MARK: In the strict scientific sense Captain, we all feed on death – even vegetarians.

The binoculars now investigate LUCY.

LUCY: Oh God. Here we go. Mark, stop it. Oh, fuck off!

MARK: (*Mimic.*) Please replace the handset and try again.

MARK puts the binoculars down and exits.

LUCY: All fucking day.

ANNA: I'll say this for your brother. He's got a nice cock.

ANNA smiles then starts to laugh. So does LUCY. LUCY photographs ANNA laughing.

Sound and on screen, the sixth face: JOY.

LUCY: I'd say that's joy.

ANNA looks at the screen.

ANNA: Yeah.

LUCY: You can thank me later.

ANNA: You're going to be in so much trouble.

LUCY: Chill out. He'll be fine.

ANNA: Let's just get your brother dressed.

LUCY: (*Little laugh.*) Yeah.

ANNA: You look for his clothes. I'll try to find the phone.

Scene 4

STEPHEN's room. STEPHEN enters carrying the glass that ANNA threw at LUCY. He is rehearsing an important lecture. He looks at the six faces on the screen.

STEPHEN: The face. The most compelling object in the social universe. Newborn babies prefer faces to any other visual stimulus. Within two weeks a child will mirror the movements of its mother's eyes and lips. Faces signal a plethora of vital information. Bone structure and skin texture announce our sex, identity, age and attractiveness. Shifts of expression and gaze reveal our moods and intentions, sometimes despite all our efforts to conceal them. Because we are not only hard-wired to respond to faces. We are hard-wired to read them.

Referring to ANNA's six faces.

Six expressions of emotion. Six thin slices of behaviour frozen in time. Fear, anger, sadness, joy, surprise, and…

STEPHEN spits into the glass.

…disgust. The basic flavours of feeling. The list by no means exhausts the repertoire of human emotion. We might add wonder and awe. We might add shame and guilt. And what life is worth living without love? But these six: Anger, fear, joy, sadness, surprise and, disgust – are primordial. Innate. Basic. Universal.

STEPHEN spits into the glass.

But what is an emotion? In one sense no more than a co-ordinated pattern of changes in behaviour and bodily function: different configurations of the facial musculature; (*He demonstrates.*) musculoskeletal responses; (*He flinches, postures as if to fight, then droops his shoulders in sadness.*) and expressive vocalisations… (*He demonstrates this by vocalising 'Aahh' with different emotional tones. Pauses to reflect.*) No. No! Don't do the actions Stephen. You'll look like a cunt.

STEPHEN spits into the glass.

We share the basic emotions with the great apes and other mammals and yet they are so central to *human* experience. They make us what we are. They give our lives meaning; make life worth living, or perhaps ending.

STEPHEN considers the glass of spit.

They raise us to the pinnacle of spiritual and artistic experience. They do all this. And yet in the end, it all comes down to biology.

STEPHEN swills the glass and drinks the contents.

Ahh. Disgusting.

But does it then follow that we are merely the puppets of our emotions?

MARK, now partially dressed (and still at ANNA's therefore unseen by STEPHEN) runs across the stage. He grabs the puppet and runs off.

ANNA: Mark no! You'll break it! Mark! Come back!

ANNA almost exits after him.

Jesus Christ! LUCY! LUCY! Mark's on the roof!

LUCY runs across the stage.

LUCY: Calm down!

ANNA: I told you Lucy! I told you!

LUCY: CALM DOWN! He does it all the time. He's not scared of anything. He's fearless. You stay here and I'll get him down.

LUCY exits after MARK.

ANNA wants to kill or shout at LUCY but stops as if pulled in too many directions.

ANNA: Ahhhhh!

STEPHEN: 'There is nothing either good or bad, but thinking makes it so.' Shakespeare's profound insight into the nature of the relationship between human thought and emotion anticipates the development of Cognitive Behavioural Therapy by nearly four centuries.

ANNA lights a cigarette and smokes deeply.

And this single brilliant line from *Hamlet* – 'There is nothing either good or bad but thinking makes it so' – encapsulates the very essence of the approach.

STEPHEN again spits into the glass. ANNA looks at her cigarette. It's dirty.

ANNA: Ugh.

ANNA puts her cigarette in the glass STEPHEN is holding, grabs a cloth and wipes her hands as she exits. STEPHEN looks at the glass.

STEPHEN: No. Once is enough.

STEPHEN puts the glass down.

The way we think about things, the way we interpret our thoughts, determines how we feel and behave. What a beautiful idea that is. So simple we don't appreciate how important it is. Like we never think about the air we breathe.

So drag your dread thoughts from the dark and hold them to the light. Inspect them. Turn them. See them this way and that. Tame them. And thus by mastering thought you master emotion.

MARK: (*Off and shouting.*) Are you out of your Vulcan mind?!

LUCY: (*Off and shouting.*) Stand still!

MARK enters trying to escape LUCY. He is pulling off his clothes. LUCY is trying to make him put them back on.

STEPHEN: What's going on?

LUCY: For fuck's sake!

STEPHEN: Lucy!

MARK: Insults are effective only where emotion is present.

LUCY: Fuck you Mark!

STEPHEN: Lucy! What's happened?

MARK: (*Mimic.*) He's called Brian!

LUCY: He just freaked out at Anna's. He climbed out on the roof.

STEPHEN: The roof? Mark, you know the rule.

MARK: He's called Brian!

STEPHEN: Who's Brian?

LUCY: No idea. Shut up. Idiot.

STEPHEN: What happened Mark? Why did you climb on the roof?

MARK: (*Fast. During this MARK will clam down into a rocking motion.*) Quite simply Captain, I examined the problem from all angles, and it was plainly hopeless. Logic informed me that under the circumstances, the only logical action would have to be one of desperation. A logical decision, logically arrived at.

STEPHEN: What did you do Lucy?

LUCY: Why is it always my fault? Look Dad, you're going to have to look after him. I have to go to rehearsals.

STEPHEN: You said you were free this afternoon.

LUCY: They changed the schedule.

STEPHEN: No Lucy, you promised.

LUCY: It's not my fault.

STEPHEN: No. I've got to get this finished. You know how important this is.

LUCY: Shit happens Dad. There's nothing I can do about it. Sorry. I have to go.

LUCY exits.

STEPHEN: Lucy!

MARK: (*Makes the sound of static.*) That sound was the turbulence caused by the penetration of a boundary layer, Captain.

STEPHEN: (*Exasperation.*) Ugh.

MARK: A boundary layer between what and what Mr Spock?

STEPHEN: Mark. Stop it. Please, just get the telescope out.

MARK: It's not eight o'clock.

STEPHEN: Mark.

MARK: A boundary layer between where we were and where we are, Captain.

STEPHEN: (*Looking at MARK.*) This is not to say that thought alone leads to intelligent action. Consider Mr Spock, the half human, half Vulcan from *Star Trek*. Behind his humanoid face sits an alien brain. Far superior to our own apparently – because the Vulcans dispensed with emotion. Leaving only superhuman rationality. But take away emotion and you take away survival. Because without anger, a child will be victimised mercilessly. Without disgust, he will eat his own shit. And without fear he will climb on rooftops, slip, laugh and calmly fall to a horrible death. Like a fucking idiot. Won't he Mark?

MARK: Like a fucking idiot.

STEPHEN: No, no, you are not an idiot Mark. (*To self.*) That's the fucking tragedy.

MARK: Are you trying to be funny, Mr Spock? It would never occur to me, Captain.

Scene 5

ANNA's studio. ANNA is working with clay, attempting to sculpt a child's face. Behind her, on the sofa, the space-man puppet. LUCY and MARK enter. LUCY throwing her bag, coat and shoes off as she talks. MARK holds his bag.

LUCY: He's a prick.

ANNA looks at LUCY.

A complete and utter, total prick.

ANNA: Right. Hello Mark.

MARK: It's not four o'clock.

LUCY: Bastard.

ANNA: Who are we talking about?

LUCY: What do you mean? Brian of course. Cunt.

ANNA: The cinematographer?

LUCY: (*Correction.*) Cameraman.

ANNA: Right.

LUCY: Total prick fucker bastard wanker cunt. He says he wants to slow down.

ANNA: Right.

ANNA moves the puppet from the sofa to a safer place.

LUCY: He didn't want to slow down last night when I had his dick in my mouth. Well he did. But that was totally different. You're right Anna. All men are bastards.

MARK: All men are bastards.

ANNA: No they're not Mark. All men are not bastards.

MARK: It's not four o'clock.

LUCY: Yes they are. Bastards. All of them. He says I play too many games. That I'm frightened of being genuine. *Genuine.* I mean what the fuck does that mean?

ANNA: Right.

LUCY: And stop saying right.

MARK: I don't like games.

LUCY: He says I'm unreliable. That I don't stick to arrangements.

ANNA: Well…

LUCY: That I don't call when I say I'm going to… What do you mean 'well'?

ANNA: Well. You don't stick to arrangements Lucy.

MARK: We're not staying.

LUCY: Yes I do. Mostly. And if I play games sometimes what's the problem? Men like games. Don't they?

ANNA: Do you like games?

MARK: I don't like games. We're not staying.

LUCY: Whose side are you on?

ANNA: It's not about sides.

LUCY: Yes it is!

MARK: I don't like games.

ANNA looks at MARK.

LUCY: Oh for fuck's sake Mark can you just stop being you for two fucking minutes.

ANNA: Lucy!

MARK: I don't like games… I don't like games…

LUCY: Mark doesn't mind.

MARK exits.

Shit Mark! MARK!

LUCY runs to the door and out after MARK. ANNA lights a cigarette.

(*Off.*) Sorry Mark.

MARK: (*Off.*) Okay.

LUCY enters.

LUCY: He's outside. He's fine. And can you please not do that, it's disgusting. And so fucking stupid. Brian smokes.

ANNA: Of course he does.

ANNA doesn't put her cigarette out but sits down. LUCY waits and looks at ANNA, then the truth comes out.

LUCY: He has an ex-wife and a spoilt bitch of a daughter and he thinks it's going to be awkward for her because we're similar ages.

ANNA: Oh. I see.

LUCY: Awkward. Of course it's going to be *awkward.* But he won't even introduce us! He says I make him happy. Happy! And we all want the people we love to be happy, don't we? I do. So she will. If she meets me, she'll understand. Eventually. *Awkward.* He's been divorced for three years Anna. *Three* years! Coward. That's what he is. He's a coward and he dares lecture me about being *genuine.*

ANNA: Your Dad's been divorced for longer than that.

LUCY: So what?

ANNA: So… Nothing

LUCY: You said Dad's being divorced longer than Brian.

ANNA: Yes.

LUCY: So that's not nothing.

ANNA: All I meant was, is, is that your Dad hasn't started a new relationship yet and he's been divorced longer than Brian.

LUCY: Yes he has. He's always fucking his patients.

ANNA: Is he?

LUCY: I don't know. Probably. Look, I know I'm being a total bitch.

ANNA: No you're not.

LUCY: I am. I know I am. I'm being an absolute child.

Beat.

It's just… I think I love him.

ANNA: You think you love him.

LUCY: Yes. I do. I think.

MARK enters.

ANNA: Right.

LUCY: I love him, okay!

MARK: It's four o'clock.

MARK puts down his bag, takes off his coat and hat and puts his belongings in their usual place. Clearly this a well established routine.

ANNA: And have you told him?

LUCY: You really are fucking mad!

ANNA: Seriously. Lucy, if you feel this strongly. Why don't you tell him? Tell him how you feel.

LUCY: But what if he doesn't… You know?

ANNA: Yeah. Well…

MARK gets the puppet.

49

LUCY: No. You're right. Tell him. Of course you're right. I should tell him.

MARK holds the puppet out to ANNA and LUCY.

MARK: I think I love him.

Beat.

Yes. I do. I think.

Beat. Music. ANNA and LUCY exit. MARK puts the puppet down, showing no love at all.

Scene 6

STEPHEN's room.

MARK: Everything is made of atoms. The atoms in my body were made in the stars. Except for the hydrogen atoms. Hydrogen atoms are primordial. They were made in the Big Bang. At the start of the Universe. Helium is primordial too. But there is no helium in my body.

MARK's feet take him to get the telescope. ANNA enters and watches. MARK turns round, and sees her and stops.

(*Agitated.*) That sound was the turbulence caused by the penetration of a boundary layer, Captain. I know the rule. It was my feet.

ANNA: It's okay Mark.

MARK: It's not eight o'clock.

ANNA: No it's not. Is your Dad here?

MARK: Dad's room is private. But my feet came in so I had to come too.

ANNA: Your feet came in?

MARK: They wanted to. Then it felt nice and then I wanted the telescope. Are you still sad?

ANNA: Sad?

MARK: Lucy said you were sad.

ANNA: Well… I'm not sure. Do I look sad?

MARK: I don't know.

Beat.

I have trouble with faces.

ANNA: Do you?

MARK: Yes.

ANNA: Me too.

MARK: You too.

ANNA: Yes.

MARK: It's a problem with my emotion circuits. Dad says.

ANNA sort of smiles and sits down.

My emotion circuits are not connected properly. My amygdala is faulty and everything gets through the hippocampus and fills my brain, which is bigger than normal. It's a whopper. Except for my cerebellum, which isn't. So I remember everything but I don't get the feelings right. Or the actions. Dad says.

ANNA: Does he now? And what's your theory?

MARK: There's also a problem with the flow of information between the two hemispheres of my brain. My thought processes get stuck in the left hemisphere, which is why I like analyzing things and why I get upset if things get out of order. But it makes me anxious and jumpy if it gets over active.

ANNA: And how do you fix that?

MARK: You have to unblock the corpus callosum.

ANNA: What's that?

MARK: The corpus callosum is the main channel of communication between the two sides of the brain. It contains 200 million axonal fibres. Approximately.

ANNA: Oh.

MARK: It gets blocked. So I have to unblock it.

ANNA: And how do you do that?

MARK: Masturbation.

Beat.

ANNA: Right… Gosh. And masturbation…

MARK: Unblocks the corpus callosum.

ANNA: Well…fascinating.

MARK: Then I feel better.

ANNA: Have you ever thought of getting a girlfriend, Mark?

MARK: I haven't got the central processing capacity. Too many hidden variables. I haven't got the computing power.

ANNA: Relationships are too complicated.

MARK: People.

Beat.

ANNA: Do you love your father, Mark?

MARK: He thinks I'm an idiot.

ANNA: And what do you think about him?

MARK: I think he's tall.

ANNA: Oh.

MARK: And he likes *Star Trek*. I like stars more than *Star Trek*.

ANNA: Stars don't have feelings. Or actions.

MARK: There are a hundred billion stars in the galaxy. Approximately. There are a hundred billion galaxies in the universe.

Enter STEPHEN.

STEPHEN: And a hundred billion neurons in the brain. Approximately. Oh hello.

ANNA: Sorry, I'm early. Lucy let me in.

MARK: It would take a hundred billion baked beans to fill the Albert Hall.

STEPHEN: Approximately.

MARK: Approximately.

STEPHEN: It's not eight o'clock yet Mark.

MARK: No it's not.

STEPHEN: Tell your feet to take you out of here son.

MARK: Yes Dad.

MARK looks at his feet.

They're not listening.

STEPHEN gently pushes his son towards the door. MARK reacts with a sound, but starts moving.

STEPHEN: Doesn't like being touched.

MARK: Live long and prosper Dad.

STEPHEN: Live long and prosper son.

Exit MARK. ANNA sits as does STEPHEN.

Sorry.

ANNA: It's okay.

STEPHEN: So. How are you?

ANNA: Okay.

STEPHEN: Good.

ANNA: No. Not good. Not good at all. Something happened last night.

STEPHEN: Last night?

ANNA: In the studio. Something... This is going to sound ridiculous... em...

STEPHEN: Go on.

ANNA: Look. There's one thing you don't do – never do – ever – is step over a puppet. You just don't.

STEPHEN: Superstition?

ANNA: Respect. Well, yes, of course superstition but it's more than that. It's a breach…

STEPHEN: A breach?

ANNA: Really. A sacrilege. I know. I know…

STEPHEN: Magical thinking.

ANNA: Magical thinking?

STEPHEN: Investing objects with emotional, psychological significance. Wedding rings, teddy bears. Puppets.

ANNA: Well, yes then. In a way, I suppose. No, yes, exactly. That is puppetry. Magical thinking. Projecting life into a dead thing…

Beat.

STEPHEN: And you stepped over one?

ANNA: Yes.

STEPHEN: And it's troubling you.

ANNA: I apologised.

STEPHEN: To the puppet?

ANNA: Yes. Then I hung her back on the wall. You know. Away from me. Went back to her face. Don't know why. Sat down. But couldn't settle. Because I can't… Couldn't, em… I was holding the scalpel and looking at the mould… but I couldn't… Couldn't focus. Couldn't em… Tried to write them down. But the noises. The thoughts.

STEPHEN: Good.

ANNA: No. Not good.

STEPHEN: Yes, Anna. Good.

ANNA: No. Not good. Not *my* thoughts.

STEPHEN: Meaning?

ANNA: Meaning *not my fucking thoughts,* Stephen!

STEPHEN is taken aback by her ferocity.

I'm sorry.

STEPHEN: Not *your* thoughts? Whose?

ANNA: From another time. Another. From another me. And I was looking for my pen, to write them down, to write and I had my book and the scalpel slipped or, well it just slipped and I, I don't know and it…it cut my arm. It didn't hurt. Just some blood, and it didn't hurt at all, and the blood, a little, some, not, you know, and then I just looked up and her.

STEPHEN: Her? The puppet?

ANNA: And she was looking back at me. But she doesn't have a face Stephen. Just a body, and I… I don't know how but she'd managed to turn round, I mean, she didn't…but she must have swung or something, the way I hung her back on the hook, or…but somehow she'd moved and was just hanging there, looking at me, and I had blood on my arm and on the…she was…and I could see her face, imagine it, no, *see it,* pushed up against the wall. Pretending it was normal. Her little face, that I can't even carve… I just can't, but I could see her and she was smiling at me. Full of…of joy and then I heard these sounds and I realised I was crying. (*Starts to laugh.*) Sobbing actually. I mean really sobbing, you know… And I got up and I went to her and said thank you and I turned her body back. Against the wall. And then I just cleaned myself up.

STEPHEN: And did she answer you?

ANNA: What?

STEPHEN: When you apologised. When you thanked her. Did the puppet reply?

ANNA: Reply? Well. Yes she did. Yes. And we had a great chat actually, I told her all about my suicidal fantasies, she told me about her wooden leg. Giving her terrible trouble apparently.

STEPHEN looks at ANNA.

No. She didn't reply.

STEPHEN: Oh.

ANNA: Which is a good thing. I take it.

STEPHEN: (*Smiles.*) Yes.

ANNA looks at STEPHEN.

Beat.

Your suicidal fantasies?

ANNA: I was joking Stephen.

STEPHEN: Oh. I see. And it was when you went back to carve her face, that's when the scalpel slipped?

ANNA: Stop fucking with my head Stephen. I know what triggers them. The thoughts. Of course I know... But it doesn't help. Knowing doesn't help. Nothing can. Nothing! Ugh, this is crap. Crap! Turn my negative thoughts into positive thoughts and I too will be happy! Always look on the bright side. Let's all be happy. It's all such bollocks! I've read the books Stephen, and I know the theories. I have read hundreds of books, a whole library on the subject. Well not hundreds. I'm exaggerating. Tens. I have read tens of books. A small library.

STEPHEN: It's one thing to understand emotions conceptually and quite another to experience them...

ANNA: I will not be patronised by you just because you're clever.

STEPHEN: I'm not patronising you Anna.

ANNA: No?

STEPHEN: No.

ANNA: Good. (*Hard.*) Because you can't be that clever if your spoilt bitch of a daughter is anything to go by.

Beat.

Sorry. Shit! I didn't mean that…

STEPHEN: It's okay.

ANNA: It's not okay. It's not *okay*. This is what it's like. What I'm like. All the time. I keep seeing that face Stephen.

STEPHEN: The puppet?

ANNA: I just keep seeing it.

STEPHEN: The puppet without a face?

ANNA: All the time. Everywhere. At night. In the dark.

STEPHEN: It's not unusual to see faces, Anna, to imagine them, especially at night-time as you're dropping off to sleep. There's a word for it: hypnogogic imagery.

ANNA: Don't toy with me. Stop pretending this is normal. This is not *normal*. There is something inside me not right. Not right…lying awake listening to things, sounds in the room, from the dark, sounds in my head, my heart pumping. The prayer. What terrible thoughts to fill a child's head with.

STEPHEN: And what thoughts does it trigger?

ANNA: *Thought.* One thought. Death.

STEPHEN: Death? Is that what this is all about? Fear of death?

ANNA: (*Calmly, quite brightly.*) Actually, no.

Beat.

No. I want to die. Get it over with. If I were dead I wouldn't be afraid any more, would I? (*Laughs.*) Now that is mad, Stephen isn't it? A mad thought if ever there was one. But if there aren't any positives to block the negatives. If there's no good thought to bash the bad thought away, well, why not a mad thought? Isn't the thought of death as negative as it gets. No positive reply to that, is there? No happy-clappy-look-on-the-bright-side-cognitive-therapy-stuff to work with when it comes to oblivion. Just platitudes.

STEPHEN: Well…

ANNA: Well what? No. Go on. Go on. Thought: 'One day I'll be dead.' Counter-thought: …well, Stephen? What's the counter-thought?

STEPHEN: I am alive still. *Now.* Awareness of the reality of death enriches my sense of being alive, now, in the moment.

ANNA: Wow. That's brilliant Doc. Never thought of that! Fuck, I think I'm cured! What do I owe you?

ANNA rummages in her bag.

Can I have one of these? (*Cigarette.*) Am I allowed to smoke in here? I'm sure I'm not, you're not allowed to smoke anywhere any more, which is good. (*Lighting up.*) Cigarettes are shit. The bastards. And I don't really want one really. They're disgusting. But I'm nervous. I really don't want this. Shit. (*Stubs out cigarette and throws it, her packet of cigarettes and her lighter in the bin.*) Talking to your best friend's father about…you know. Seeing you differently I mean. Do you see me differently? This is not easy for me. And I love Lucy. I do and I'd do anything for her, more, and she's been… I didn't want to come to see you, you know. It was Lucy who got me here. Lucy… And maybe she's right about my work, maybe my work *is* too personal, maybe I do give too much to the puppets, and they do take a lot out of me, to vitalise them, to bring them to life and to listen to what they want, you know, but I love my work, more than anything and I can't imagine not doing it, can't, and if it comes to a choice between being cured and my work well then fuck being cured frankly, my work is all I have, and I'm not going to give it up, I'm not. *Never.*

Beat.

STEPHEN: (*Unheard by ANNA.*) I want to fuck you Anna.

ANNA: Why did Catherine leave you?

Awkward moment.

Why did Catherine leave you and Lucy?

STEPHEN: And Mark.

ANNA: And Mark. Did she leave because of Mark?

Beat.

Sorry.

STEPHEN: She fell in love.

ANNA: (*Surprise.*) Oh.

STEPHEN: It happens.

ANNA: Sorry. I thought it was… With a patient. I thought. Don't you always sleep with your patients? Sorry. I can't control myself… I keep… What am I doing? You see! I don't know what the fuck I'm doing.

ANNA lights another cigarette.

STEPHEN: (*Unheard by ANNA.*) I'm not embarrassed by the question Anna. It's strange to admit. But I'm going to be honest with you, because I don't think I'm going to be able to help you. Professionally I mean, because…because since the moment you came here, to see me, since the moment you walked through the door, I *have* seen you differently…

ANNA takes a hanky and blows her nose. STEPHEN embarks on a
fantasy, unheard by ANNA, self-editing his thoughts as he goes.

You sit there, vulnerable and open, asking for my help,
and I don't want to help, because in my mind, I'm… No.
Don't… Oh, fuck. Oh, Jesus *fuck.* Look at you. I want
to feel your breath on my mouth…touching you… I'm
exploring you, tasting you. As soon as I saw you, Anna.
The *moment* I saw you. Your mouth. I'm watching your
mouth. You talk and I don't hear what you're saying.
No, I *do.* I'm a professional. I *register* what you're saying.
Your words run through my brain. I register. I respond.
I nod sagely, sympathetically. I cock my head. Empathy,
genuineness and warmth. I listen. I'm an expert listener.
I cock my head. My cock in your head. (*A choked laugh
– disguised as a cough – at the absurd conjunction*.). Oh,
Stephen, fuck off. Fuck *OFF!* In your mouth, my cock
in your mouth. Your lush hair brushing my skin. Your
lips working…wetly, taking my cock, sucking…as you
speak…fucking your mouth. As you speak, Anna, as you
speak. Sucking my cock. Oo-oh, God, yes. My straining
cock… *Straining cock!* This is third-rate porn… So what?
So fucking what? It's okay to think. Isn't it? Mental
rape. No? No. She's consenting. So. Fine… But she's not
consenting to you thinking about her consenting is she? It
be the gentlemanly thing to ask permission. Permission?
Oh, God, look at you. Those little flashes of pink tongue
as you speak. That tongue licking my…the end of my
cock…my Hamlet… Hamlet? Helmet! Your mouth is…
Fucking *helmet!* (*Shakes his head almost irritated. Then gets
quickly back on track.*) And I'm coming. And you're sucking
and swallowing. I just keep coming. Your mouth is open,
open, my come on your lips, on your tongue…you look…
Disgusted?… No… Yes… Yes! Disgusted with greed
for more…

ANNA: I'm sorry. I shouldn't have said that.

STEPHEN: No.

ANNA: I am. It's absolutely none of my business.

STEPHEN: Intrusive thoughts. We all have them. There's no need to apologise. We're going to work this out.

STEPHEN stands. The session is over. ANNA stands, looks at STEPHEN then exits. STEPHEN looks down. Then up. He is somehow distracted. He pulls a handful of tissues from the box. Turns his back on us and starts to masturbate.

Anna... I know this is wrong... Not strictly... Well, not at all... But... You're the most...most, beautiful, beautiful... Your mouth... Take me. Take me. Don't stop. Take me. Don't stop. Please don't stop. Anna. Ahh. Anna. Anna. Ughh. Ugh. Uuuh.

STEPHEN has dropped the hankies and comes in his hand. ANNA re-enters. STEPHEN hides his hand behind his back.

ANNA: Okay. I'm not sorry.

STEPHEN: Well... Good.

ANNA: Thank you Stephen. For listening.

STEPHEN: It's my job.

ANNA: I know, but...thanks.

STEPHEN: Okay.

ANNA exits. MARK's feet bring MARK on upstage. STEPHEN picks up the hankies and wipes his hands, then he throws them into the bin and exits. It is impossible to tell from MARK's expression what he has heard or what he is thinking.

MARK: (*Uninflected.*) Anna... I know this is wrong... Not strictly... Well, not at all... But... You're the most...most, beautiful, beautiful... Your mouth... Take me. Take me. Don't stop. Take me. Don't stop. Please don't stop. Anna. Ahh. Anna. Anna. Ughh. Ugh. Uuuh.

Enter LUCY, worried.

LUCY: Mark! Are you all right Mark? What's wrong?

MARK: Nothing.

LUCY: You were crying.

MARK: No I wasn't.

LUCY: Yes you were.

MARK: I was acting.

LUCY: Acting? Are you taking the piss?

MARK: Act to feel Lucy. And joy will follow.

LUCY: Right. Well come on, you better get out of here. You know the rules.

MARK: Dad's room is private. Don't climb on the roof.

LUCY: So come on. Get out.

MARK: It's eight o'clock. Dun Dun Da! Time to look through the telescope.

LUCY: Well Dad's not here Mark so you're going to have to wait.

MARK: (*Getting agitated.*) The release of emotion is what keeps us healthy. Emotionally healthy.

LUCY: (*Almost shouting.*) Mark, just get out of Dad's room!

MARK: That may be Doctor. However I have noted that the healthy release of emotion is frequently unhealthy for those closest to you. It's eight o'clock!

LUCY: Mark. Tell your fucking feet to take you out of Dad's room.

MARK looks at his feet. They don't move.

LUCY pushes her brother, fairly violently, out of the room. He starts to have a panic attack.

MARK: That sound was the penetration of a boundary layer Captain! It's eight o'clock! It's eight o'clock! It's eight o'clock...!

MARK exits. We hear his tantrum continuing. LUCY waits until he has calmed down or gone then takes her phone out, looks at it, thinks then decides to call Brian. She lets it ring three times then changed her mind and ends the call. Then she decides to call ANNA. There are three unheard rings.

LUCY: Hi Anna. It's me. Lucy. Sorry. It's just em...

LUCY tries to smile.

She baked me a cake.

LUCY starts crying but doesn't want ANNA to know so she covers the phone then disguises her tears as laughter. ANNA's lines are unheard by the audience.

ANNA:

LUCY: She baked me a cake.

ANNA:

LUCY: A cake. (*Serious.*) Can you believe that?

ANNA:

LUCY: Brian's daughter. He introduced us last night.

ANNA:

LUCY: Yeah. I met her. And she'd baked me a cake.

LUCY becomes extremely upset again but pulls herself together.

ANNA:

LUCY: It was delicious. It was totally delicious.

ANNA:

LUCY: Honestly. It was the most delicious cake I have ever tasted. And I'm not exaggerating. What am I going to do?

ANNA:

> *LUCY covers the phone.*

LUCY: What am I going to do Anna?

> *LUCY takes a deep breath and then talks into the phone.*

Sorry. I'm over-reacting as usual. Just being really dramatic.

ANNA:

LUCY: Yeah. I'm fine. I'm fine. How are you? You seeing Dad later?

ANNA:

LUCY: Well good. Keep up the good work.

ANNA:

LUCY: Yeah. Okay. Sorry Anna. Mark's calling me. Got to go. Love you. Bye. Bye.

> *LUCY hangs up, starts crying again then almost immediately pulls herself together. She looks at her phone, presses a button to phone Brian. Waits... She lets it ring three times then changes her mind and ends the call.*

Scene 7

STEPHEN's room. STEPHEN is rehearsing his lecture. Making corrections and notes as he goes. MARK is looking through the telescope, making his own notes.

STEPHEN: *Cognitive dissonance.* Again, it's a simple idea. We feel a kind of uncomfortable tension when our thoughts conflict with one another. 'I'm a young woman. I can sleep with an older man if I choose to. No problem. But then. My best friend is sleeping with my father. Problem.' But why?

'I'm an older man. I can sleep with a young woman if I choose to. No problem.' That's cool. *Cool?* Have you started saying *cool?* 'But then the woman I want to sleep with is my client. Well that's altogether different. Problem.' Big problem. Professional problem. Family problem. Totally *un-cool.* Oh Jesus, get a grip.

But Cognitive Dissonance is more than just conflicting thoughts. And this is where I depart from the standard explanations… Because I believe that dissonance is built in to us. And rooted in emotion.

Our brains have two quite distinct moral evaluation systems: One we know. And it's the one we're proud of: Our conscious thought, our reason. But the other is hidden. Lurks beneath consciousness. Devious. Primitive. Powerful. Our emotional system.

And, when these two systems come into conflict we experience a… a kind of… we are dumbfounded… *morally dumbfounded…* Because we think we use reason to make moral judgements, when in fact the conclusions we reach are pre-set at gut level. That's it.

(*STEPHEN smiles.*) Consider the following scenario: a man goes to the supermarket and buys an oven-ready chicken. Gets it home, slips on a condom, and has sex with it. And then he cooks it and serves it to his friends for dinner.

What? What's wrong with that? No one is any the wiser.
The meat is uncontaminated. It's well cooked. And with a
little garlic. Mmm. Delicious.

Innocent shrug.

Scenario two: one day, after a nice chicken dinner, our
friend and his sister decide they would like to have sex
together.

Beat. Mock surprise.

Just the *once*. So they do. Enjoyably. Using contraception,
and agreeing to keep it a secret. It's a beautiful, one-off
experience that enhances their relationship. So is it wrong?
No one got hurt.

So it's okay to fuck a chicken. Jesus Christ Stephen. And
your sister! They're going to think you're a complete
pervert. Okay. Look. Well, we can probably all agree such
behaviour is degrading. And that we shouldn't do it. But
why shouldn't we do it? What's the reason?

The fact is, most people can't give a convincing reason.
They are morally dumbfounded – knowing intuitively
that something is wrong but being stuck for a rational
justification. And the reason for this dumbfounding is our
two moral evaluation systems: We think we use reason
to make moral judgements, when actually we're allowing
ourselves to be puppeted – sneakily puppeted – by our
emotions.

Beat as MARK thinks.

MARK: It's okay to fuck a chicken.

STEPHEN: Sorry son? What did you say?

MARK: It's okay to fuck a chicken!

STEPHEN: No. Shit! No… No it's not Mark.

MARK: It's okay to fuck a chicken!

STEPHEN: No Mark, listen to me. Listen son. *It is not okay to fuck a chicken.*

Scene 8

ANNA's studio. ANNA is standing by her sculpting easel looking at the blank face she is trying to sculpt but can't. Time passes. What is she thinking? ANNA sings.

ANNA: Now I lay me down to sleep,
    I pray the Lord my soul to keep.
    If I should die before I wake,
    I pray the Lord my soul to take.

    Now I lay me
    Now I lay me down to sleep,
    I pray the Lord my soul to keep.
    If I should die before I wake,
    I pray the Lord my soul to take.

    LUCY enters. She stands and looks at ANNA.

    Now I lay me down to sleep,
    Now I lay me down to sleep,
    Now I lay me down to sleep.

LUCY: Hi.

    ANNA looks up.

ANNA: Oh. Hi. Is it four o'clock?

LUCY: Nearly. He's outside. How's the portrait?

ANNA: Em. It's not.

    LUCY sits down.

    How's Brian?

LUCY: Okay. I think. Fine.

ANNA: And his daughter?

LUCY: Yeah. She's good. Lovely.

ANNA: Malleable?

LUCY: Yeah.

ANNA smiles.

ANNA: I'm happy for you Lucy.

LUCY looks at ANNA.

I am. Really.

MARK enters.

MARK: It's four o'clock. My face in space.

MARK enters. Putting his bag, coat and hat in their usual place then he looks for the puppet.

ANNA: Hello Mark.

MARK: My face in space.

LUCY: He means the puppet. He's been talking about it all day. I said you'd teach him how to use it.

ANNA: He's not quite finished.

MARK: It's four o'clock. It's four o'clock. Dun Dun Da!

LUCY: It doesn't matter Anna.

ANNA: Yes it does.

LUCY: Mark won't mind. Just get it.

MARK: The women on your planet are logical Mr Spock? Yes Captain.

LUCY: Anna please. I can't handle any more *Star Trek.*

MARK: Does your logic find this fascinating, Mr Spock?

LUCY: Get it for fuck's sake.

ANNA gets the puppet for MARK.

MARK: Fascinating is a word I use for the unexpected. In this case, I should think interesting would suffice. (*ANNA stands the puppet up.*) You have the bridge Mr Spock. You have the bridge!

ANNA: Okay Mark. Here you take the head.

ANNA moves to give MARK the head.

MARK: Don't stand too close or you'll put her off. And make eye contact. But not like a window-licker.

LUCY laughs.

LUCY: I've been teaching him how to chat up women.

ANNA: Window-licker?

LUCY: Yeah, it's slang, you know, for spastic.

ANNA: I know what it is Lucy. You can't say things like that. Mark is not a plaything.

LUCY: It just sort of slipped out.

ANNA: You are not a window-licker Mark.

MARK: I know. I never lick windows.

LUCY laughs again.

LUCY: Maybe I should take the head. Mark might not be able to control it.

ANNA: It's not how it works.

LUCY: Yeah I know, but… Okay, okay, you're the teacher. Mark. Take the head. And his left hand. Hold it like this. I have to hold his right hand. Okay? Anna, will do the feet. Do you understand?

MARK: I'm not an idiot.

ANNA: No you're not, Mark.

LUCY takes the puppet's right hand.

LUCY: Come on Anna, show him what to do.

MARK: The head thinks. The body feels. And the feet move. It's perfectly logical.

LUCY: Well, thank you Mr Spock.

MARK: You're welcome, Captain.

ANNA: And breathing. Breathing is the key. We have to find the puppet's breath to make it come to life.

ANNA takes the feet and the three breathe together and find the puppet's breath.

Yes. That's it.

LUCY: Brilliant Mark!

The puppet moves and stops and moves again. Then:.

MARK: (*Mimicking father.*) Anna…

LUCY: So he wants to talk!

MARK: Yes.

The puppet looks down at ANNA. Then he raises his right hand.

Anna…

ANNA: Yes Mark? Come on. What does he want to say?

MARK: I know this is wrong…

ANNA: No it's not. Let him talk. It's not wrong.

MARK: Not strictly… Well, not at all… But… You're the most…most, beautiful, beautiful… Your mouth… Take me. Take me. Don't stop. Take me. Don't stop. Please don't stop. Anna. Ahh. Anna. Anna. Ughh. Ugh. Uuuh. Heee-heeee! Heee-heeee!

MARK grins like a cat.

LUCY: Where did you hear that Mark?

MARK: Dad's room is private. I know the rules.

LUCY laughs then looks at her friend.

Beat.

LUCY: (*Still smiling.*) Are you fucking my Dad?

Beat.

Are you fucking my Dad?

Beat.

Answer the question Anna.

ANNA: Lucy!

LUCY: You wouldn't. How could you? You would never. You're my best friend.

ANNA: Yes, yes I am.

LUCY: I saved your fucking life you fucked up slut!

ANNA: Can you hear what you're saying, Lucy?

LUCY: Do you suck his cock?

ANNA: Stop this. Right now.

LUCY: Do you suck my father's cock Anna? Jesus Christ. Don't answer that. Well do you? Answer my fucking question, at least do me the courtesy of answering my fucking question. You whore. You disgusting fucking total whore.

ANNA: I think you'd better go.

LUCY: You think I'd better go?

ANNA: It think it would be sensible.

LUCY: You think it would be sensible? You're fucking my father. And you think it would be *sensible* if I go?

ANNA: What's happened to you?

LUCY: Nothing's *happened*.

ANNA: Something's happened, to make you this frightened.

LUCY: I'm not *frightened*.

ANNA: You're frightened Lucy. It's why you sleep with so
    many stupid men and think it's the same as falling in love.

LUCY: I should have let you kill yourself.

ANNA: Maybe you should.

LUCY: You really are fucking mad!

ANNA: And you are a small, frightened, pathetic, little child.

LUCY: Well at least I'm not a *baby-killer!*

   *ANNA is stunned. LUCY is also clearly shocked by her loss of
   control.*

MARK: That sound was the penetration of a boundary layer,
    Captain.

   Beat.

LUCY: I'm sorry Anna. I didn't mean that. Any of it. I didn't. I
    promise. I didn't.

ANNA: Get out of my house Lucy.

LUCY: Anna please.

ANNA: Now.

LUCY: I'm pregnant.

   Beat.

   I'm pregnant Anna. And I can't even bake.

Scene 9

STEPHEN is rehearsing his lecture.

STEPHEN: In the year 2000 the Chinese artist, Zhu Yu, performed a famous piece of conceptual art at the Shanghai Arts Festival. It involved cooking and eating a human foetus. Disgusting. Abominable.

Beat.

Actually it was a series of photographs of him cooking and eating the foetus, which, he claims, he stole from a medical school. Though close scrutiny of the photographs reveals that the 'foetus' may in fact have been assembled by attaching the head of a doll to the body of a roast duck... (*To self.*)... Which is a pretty fucking disgusting concoction in its own right. What a way to make a living... (*Returning to lecture notes.*) Now the interesting thing is that Zhu claims his work is all about morality. (*Cynical.*) He claims that he's using disgust to explore morality! (*Definite.*) And he is absolutely right to do so.

Disgust is the most human of emotions... the one basic emotion we don't share with other animals... the one we have to *learn*. Children, they don't show disgust until the age of four or five. They reject bad tastes, of course – they'd pull a face if you fed them a slice of lemon – but that's simple taste aversion, which is not the same as disgust. Disgust is to do with *offensiveness*. And *that* we have to learn. ... So, for example, chocolate tastes very good but shape it like dog faeces and most adults are put off. They're disgusted. Not so two year olds. (*Makes note.*) Slide of toddler eating chocolate dog shit.

Disgust started out as guardian of the mouth, but then it diversified – became guardian of the whole body, protecting us against contamination and disease. With regard to sex for example... (*Reflects.*) ... Even to imagine eating a foetus? Is that immoral? Is that as bad as actually

75

doing it? And Anna? Every red-blooded heterosexual man imagines fucking every attractive woman he sets eyes on…virtually every unattractive woman come to think of it… I mean at least fleetingly, a fleeting nanosecond of lust…perfectly normal… With regard to sex, for example, our sense of disgust guides us to acceptable partners and acts…we have the same 'fearful curiosity' for sex that we have for food: eager to explore new sensations but holding back in fear of the new and the different…

And now, with a third evolutionary leap, disgust directs us in the cultural world. And so Mr Zhu is quite right in his exploration. Because it is not reason that guides us through the labyrinthine back streets of sex, religion and politics. It is the emotion, disgust.

Enter ANNA.

From guardian of the body to guardian of the soul.

ANNA: Hi.

STEPHEN: Hello. Come in. Sit down

ANNA rummages in her bag.

Have you written your story?

ANNA: And tackled my lists. I've been a very good girl sir, and completed all my homework.

ANNA produces her lists and a red apple which she holds out to STEPHEN.

For the teacher.

STEPHEN smiles, or is it panic? ANNA and STEPHEN stare at each other.

I'm joking Stephen. It's my supper.

ANNA takes a bite and searches in her bag for her story.

It helped to write it down. I didn't think it would. But writing it, held my thoughts in check somehow.

STEPHEN: Good.

ANNA: Shall I? (*Read…*)

STEPHEN: Please.

ANNA: Okay. Em… Right. Her face is where it all began. Her dead face. An unplayed instrument. I've been working on her face for hours. For years. I want to be happy. I want her to be happy. It's late. Gone midnight. Into the realm of faces. But I'm not tired. I'm lost. Adrift. I close my eyes. I open them. I close my eyes. I see her face. Tonight I see her clearly. Her cold fingers grip mine, guide the blade. Tonight she's coming through. At last. I close my eyes. I open them. And there she is. Her little bloodless face. Blank. Beautiful. Knowing. Palpable. And I'm stroking her. And she smiles at me. Is this it? Is it now? I don't know. But I can hope and I do hope. And the noises in my head, and the dripping in the pipes, and the fridge humming in the kitchen and all the thoughts, all the feelings, all the everything, begin to calm. Except her. Because she laughs! She laughs to give me courage. It is now. So I aim the scalpel and make the cut – The scalpel is small and very sharp – It doesn't hurt. But slides into my arm with grace. No pain. No tears. I hope and I cradle her face. A tear of blood hangs. Drops. And another. And another. I am weak. And weaker. And the breath leaves my body and enters hers. I close my eyes. I open my eyes. I feed her my breath with each drop. I close my eyes. I open my eyes. And she opens hers. And I know what she's going to say. And it's the most beautiful sound I have ever heard:

CHILD and ANNA: Now I lay me down to sleep,
I pray the Lord my soul to keep.
If I should die before I wake,
I pray the Lord my soul to take.

So I give her more of me, every drop. Everything. I give her everything I have. And I close my eyes. And as she finishes her little prayer I open my eyes for the last time and greet her with a smile. And I know the water will be dripping in the pipes and the fridge will hum in the kitchen but I can't hear them anymore because now I'm laughing too. I'm laughing and she's laughing! And that's all I can hear. No water, no humming, no thoughts, just laughter. And as I finally die I realise that for the first time in my life, I have experienced joy.

(*Forced chirpiness.*) Bet you hear a lot of these…

ANNA looks up to see STEPHEN.

Are you are welling up Stephen? Over a, what-did-you-call-it? A desensitisation exercise. I've done another one – Panadols and booze, but it wasn't nearly as much fun. I just get very sleepy then don't wake up.

ANNA looks at STEPHEN.

STEPHEN: You're trying to bring something back to life.

Is this why you make puppets?

Time passes. ANNA looks at STEPHEN, then into herself. What will she do? Does she trust him? Will she tell her real story? STEPHEN waits.

ANNA: I thought it through. Pros and cons. Good thoughts, bad thoughts. To be honest, there was very little emotion involved. The decision was clear. It didn't take long. But I waited. Took my time. And I debated. Responsibly. To make sure. It wasn't a child. It wasn't real. An embryo. A shrimp. Abortion is such a strange word, isn't it? The foetus did not have feelings. Or thoughts. Or anything. It did not have a life to abort. I did. It was the right thing to do. The only responsible choice. And so I made the appointment. 10am. And I set my alarm and I slept for the first time in three months. In the morning I woke up and I was clear. Still certain. And something else, I was happy. I got out of bed, took off my night dress and I went into the kitchen. I put on the kettle and went to open the fridge. And as I bent down, very, very suddenly, came the pain. It was, or, it must have been, tremendous. I remember trying to hold on to the fridge, but I couldn't. And when I came to, the first thing I saw was the clock on the wall. 10.35. And then I felt the wetness and the cold. And as I pulled myself away from my blood I saw my child. Lying on the kitchen floor beside me. Her tiny corpse... Her little face.

Time. ANNA is holding on very tightly.

STEPHEN: Thoughts are not actions, Anna. We musn't confuse them.

ANNA: Don't say it.

STEPHEN: Magical thinking.

ANNA: So what is it I feel bad about Stephen? The abortion that would have killed her or the miscarriage that did?

STEPHEN: (*Gently.*) Well, we should consider each in turn. Shall we? What do you think?

ANNA: I have no child Stephen.

Music. Something begins to crack open in ANNA.

STEPHEN: And that's what you want? A child.

ANNA: I have no child...

And now it breaks open. STEPHEN watches, he feels her pain.

STEPHEN: Magical thinking Anna. Confusing thoughts and real events. We can control that. You can. You can and you will.

ANNA is now totally distraught. Terrible. STEPHEN goes to ANNA and comforts her, a professional hand on her shoulder perhaps. But she grabs hold of him. She needs something to hold on to.

It wasn't your fault. It wasn't your fault. You're going to be okay. I promise... I promise...

Music continues. Time passes. Just a little less than needed.

ANNA: Oh… Oh God. Oh God! (*She laughs.*) Oh look, I've got snot all over your shirt!

STEPHEN: Doesn't matter.

STEPHEN gives ANNA some hankies.

ANNA: Isn't it your big lecture this evening?

STEPHEN: Yeah.

ANNA: Sorry.

ANNA blows her nose.

STEPHEN: I have to change anyway.

ANNA: You must be getting nervous. Do you get nervous?

STEPHEN: Sometimes.

ANNA: Your son has an interesting way of dealing with nerves. Unblocking the corpus callosum, he calls it.

STEPHEN: Does he?

ANNA: Yeah. Though I think you might know the technique already.

STEPHEN: Really?

ANNA: Well Lucy says he repeats everything he hears.

STEPHEN: Well that's true. Unfortunately.

ANNA: 'Anna… I know this is wrong… Not strictly… You're the most…most, beautiful, beautiful… Your mouth… Take me. Take me. Don't stop. Take me. Don't stop. Please don't stop. Anna. Ahh. Anna. Anna. Ughh. Ugh. Uuuh. Uuuh.' Something like that anyway. He demonstrated with one of my puppets.

STEPHEN doesn't know what he should do, so he stands up.

STEPHEN: Em… I want you to know, absolutely, that I would never ever have…

ANNA: What?

STEPHEN: Compromised our work together, anything like that. Never.

ANNA: No?

STEPHEN: No.

ANNA: Why not?

STEPHEN: Why not?

ANNA: Yes. Why not?

STEPHEN: Because. Em… Because…

ANNA: Because of Lucy?

STEPHEN: No. Em… Well. Yes. Lucy…but other things… Why not? You're asking…?

ANNA: Yes.

STEPHEN: You're asking…? Sorry. I don't understand the question.

ANNA waits.

I'm sorry. I don't know what to say. I've humiliated myself.

ANNA: No you haven't.

STEPHEN: Taken advantage.

ANNA: No.

ANNA stands up.

STEPHEN: Anna. You're in my care.

ANNA: And I feel that. I really feel that.

STEPHEN: Good.

ANNA: Yes it is good. It's really good.

STEPHEN: Good.

ANNA: It's really good.

ANNA gently kisses STEPHEN. STEPHEN gently pulls away.

STEPHEN: Em… Ha. Em… It's not that I don't want to. I do. I
do want to. Very, very, much. But I want you to come back
tomorrow more, so we can plan a way forward. Otherwise
you will go back.

*ANNA knows he is right but it is she who now feels humiliated. She
sits down. Considers for a moment then.*

ANNA: Right. So let's look at each in turn then. Abortion first.

STEPHEN: Okay.

STEPHEN sits.

ANNA: And imagine I was Lucy.

STEPHEN: Lucy?

ANNA: Yes. Just imagine. Stupidly pregnant. Angry and
frightened. Incapable of looking after myself let alone a
child. A whole life ahead of me. What would you advise
me to do? In your capacity as a therapist.

STEPHEN: Em…

ANNA: If I was Lucy. What would you tell me to do?

Scene 10

*Music. LUCY is thinking while on stage performing As You Like It.
She is dressed as an Elizabethan boy but she holds the puppet of the
spaceman. During what follows we can not work out what she is
thinking or feeling.*

LUCY: '…At which time would I, being but a moonish
youth, grieve, be effeminate, changeable, longing and
liking, proud, fantastical, apish, shallow, inconstant, full
of tears, full of smiles, for every passion something and
for no passion truly anything, as boys and women are for
the most part cattle of this colour; would now like him,
would now loathe him; then entertain him, then forswear
him, now weep for him, then spit at him; that I drave my
suitor from his mad humour of love to a living humour
of madness, which was to forswear the full stream of the
world and to live in a nook merely monastic. And thus I
cured him, and this way will I take upon me to wash your
liver as clean as a sound sheep's heart, that there shall not
be one spot of love in't.'

*Lights change on LUCY. She freezes. STEPHEN enters. He is holding
MARK's binoculars though does not look through them. Instead he
looks at his daughter.*

STEPHEN: The face. The most compelling object in the social
universe… Faces signal a plethora of vital information…
Shifts of expression and gaze reveal our moods and
intentions, sometimes despite all our efforts to conceal
them. Because we are not only hard-wired to respond to
faces. We are hard-wired to read them.

*MARK enters and goes to look through the telescope. STEPHEN looks
at his son, who looks back at him. They are both unable to read each
other's faces. MARK becomes slightly agitated.*

MARK: That sound was the penetration of a boundary layer
Captain.

MARK looks through the telescope. Lights change. LUCY exits.

Scene 11

STEPHEN's room. MARK is still looking through the telescope. STEPHEN looks through the binoculars.

STEPHEN: It's cloudy tonight Mark. We might not see anything.

MARK: It's *extremely* cloudy tonight Dad. But the stars are out there.

STEPHEN: There are a hundred billion stars in the galaxy. Approximately.

MARK: There are a hundred billion galaxies in the universe. Approximately.

STEPHEN: And a hundred billion neurons in the brain.

MARK: Approximately.

STEPHEN: Yeah. Approximately.

MARK: It would take a hundred billion baked beans to fill the Albert Hall. Approximately.

STEPHEN: And imagine – each baked bean a galaxy.

MARK looks up from the telescope and looks at STEPHEN as if he is an idiot. STEPHEN is still looking through the binoculars. MARK looks at the sky.

MARK: My body is made of atoms from the stars.

STEPHEN: Except for the hydrogen atoms.

MARK: Hydrogen atoms are primordial. They were made in the Big Bang. At the start of the Universe. Helium is primordial too. But there is no helium in my body. I am recycled star dust. Mostly.

MARK looks back through the telescope. A moment later STEPHEN looks at his son. Is MARK ever aware of the poetry he sometimes speaks?

Look!

STEPHEN: What?

MARK: Look Dad! Look!

STEPHEN: I can't see it Mark. What is it?

MARK: There! There!

MARK points to the telescope. STEPHEN puts the binoculars down and looks through the telescope. MARK picks up the binoculars and looks through them.

STEPHEN: The madenliest star.

MARK: That's no star. That's Jupiter. That's Jupiter!

STEPHEN looks through the telescope. MARK through his binoculars.

Can you see the stardust?

STEPHEN: (*Struck.*) Yes. Yes I can.

MARK: Jupiter is the fifth planet from the sun and the largest planet in our Solar system. Jupiter is 1,317 times the volume of earth and is primarily composed of hydrogen with a small portion of helium.

STEPHEN: Set a course for Jupiter Mr Spock.

MARK: Jupiter's outer atmosphere is divided into bands at different latitudes, resulting in turbulence and storms along their boundary layers. A prominent result is a giant dust storm. Dun Dun Da! The Great Red Spot.

Enter LUCY.

STEPHEN: Mark's just found Jupiter.

LUCY: Great Mark. Is that the one with the rings?

STEPHEN: No, that's Saturn. Jupiter's the one with the Red Spot.

MARK: Dun Dun Da!

STEPHEN: Is everything okay?

LUCY: Well?

STEPHEN: Well what?

LUCY: 'There is nothing either good or bad but thinking makes it so' How was the lecture?

STEPHEN: Oh. Yes. Yes it was fine. How was the play?

LUCY: It was *fine*? Oh Dad. You really are shit.

LUCY's phone rings. She looks for it and answers it. STEPHEN looks at his daughter.

Sorry.

MARK: Is that the one with the rings?

LUCY: Sorry Dad, It's Anna. Where are you? Em…yeah okay. Hold on.

STEPHEN: Are you okay love?

LUCY: Yeah. Fine. Why are you being weird?

STEPHEN: No. I was just asking…

LUCY: Well stop it.

STEPHEN: (*Smiling.*) Okay.

LUCY: Anna's outside. I'll go and let her in.

LUCY exits.

MARK: *Is that the one with the rings?*

STEPHEN chuckles.

Beat.

What a fucking idiot!

MARK grins at STEPHEN. STEPHEN laughs out loud.

Enter LUCY with ANNA.

LUCY: What's so funny?

STEPHEN: Em… Nothing. Just something your brother said. Hello.

ANNA: Hi.

STEPHEN: Hi.

ANNA: Hello Mark.

LUCY: Anna has a present for you Mark.

ANNA: Well it's for all of you really. Here you go.

ANNA hands the box out to MARK. MARK looks at ANNA.

STEPHEN: Well that's very sweet of you. What do you say Mark? When you're given a present, what do you say?

MARK: It's okay to fuck a chicken.

MARK takes the box.

LUCY: What did he just say?

STEPHEN: No it's not Mark.

LUCY: It's okay to fuck a chicken?

STEPHEN: No it's not okay to fuck a chicken!

LUCY: That is so sick. Dad, I can't believe you. I think you should go and see someone.

MARK unties the ribbon and opens the box. He can't believe his eyes.

MARK: You have the bridge Mr Spock! You have the bridge!

MARK holds the finished puppet up. It's of him as a spaceman. In a space suit complete now complete with a visor.

STEPHEN: Anna. It's beautiful. And look Mark. It's you.

MARK: It's my face.

STEPHEN: Yes. It's your face in there.

MARK: It's my face.

STEPHEN: And what a handsome fellow you are! Anna, it's wonderful.

ANNA: Your face. In space.

It's so you can go into space. Do you remember how to use it?

MARK: I know the rules. The head thinks, the body feels, the feet move. It's perfectly logical.

ANNA: I thought you could show your Dad Lucy. And the three of you could, you know.

LUCY: Yeah. Thanks.

MARK: I hold the head and the right arm. Like this. Lucy holds the right hand.

Beat.

LUCY holds the right hand.

STEPHEN: Maybe you should take the head Lucy. Mark might not be able to control it.

LUCY: It's not how it works Dad.

LUCY takes the puppet's right hand.

MARK: And Anna takes the feet.

ANNA: Stephen you should do it.

STEPHEN: What?

MARK: And Anna takes the feet.

LUCY: Come on Dad. Don't be frightened.

MARK: I'm not frightened!

STEPHEN: Okay, Mark. I'm taking the feet.

MARK: You're frightened Lucy.

LUCY: Mark. Stop it.

MARK: It's why you sleeps with so many stupid men and think it's the same as falling in love.

LUCY: Shut the fuck up you fucking spastic!

STEPHEN: Lucy!

MARK: I should have let you kill yourself!

STEPHEN: What?

MARK: You are a small, frightened, pathetic, little child.

STEPHEN: What's going on here?

MARK: Well at least I'm not a *baby killer!*

MARK grins.

STEPHEN: What did you say son?

MARK: At least I'm not a *baby killer!*

Beat.

STEPHEN: I'm so sorry Anna.

ANNA is looking at LUCY. STEPHEN looks at ANNA, then follows her stare to LUCY. LUCY is looking at ANNA.

Beat.

Will someone please tell me what's going on here?

STEPHEN looks at the two women.

ANNA: I should go.

LUCY: No. Stay. Please.

STEPHEN: Lucy?

STEPHEN looks at his daughter.

Music.

Scene 13

Out of time. ANNA looks at her six faces projected on the up stage screen. STEPHEN sits in his therapists' chair. LUCY stands where she was at the end of the previous scene.

MARK: (*To audience.*) And that was the night I fell off the roof.

MARK overturns the sofa to act as the roof, then lifts the puppet up on the sofa to represent him and the rest of his story.

I shouldn't have been on the roof. I know the rules. Dad's room is private. Never climb on the roof. Don't masturbate in front of Lucy.

The puppet looks at the stars.

I like the stars more than anything else. Stars don't have feelings.

Music changes.

These are the voyages of the star ship, Enterprise. Its five year mission: to explore strange new worlds… To seek out new life and new civilisations… To boldly go where no man has gone before…

(*Mimicking LUCY and making the puppet look as if he can see a tiny LUCY on the ground beneath him.*) Marks on the roof! Mark's on the roof! Get down you fucking idiot! Sorry Mark, you're not a fucking idiot. (*The puppet looks up. MARK speaks as himself.*) And then I fell off the roof. (*The puppet looks at MARK.*) What a fucking idiot.

Now the puppet jumps into space, until suddenly he falls to the ground. MARK cradles the puppet like a foetus. A one-man version of the three-person image from Scene 1.

STEPHEN concludes his lecture to the audience.

STEPHEN: Imagine if you could switch them off. Just flick a little switch in your brain and voilà. Gone the pain. Gone the tongue-tied embarrassment. Gone the overly-aggressive reply. All of these things gone. In the flick of a little switch. Just imagine if you could turn them off.

Beat.

But before you do. Remember. Gone too laughter. Gone too tears. Because no feelings of attachment would remain. The crooked little smile of the one we love would leave no trace on our heart. That moment of silliness would pass unmarked. That look. The naughty flicker through the eyes. Would mean nothing. Just imagine if you could turn them off.

STEPHEN asks the puppet.

What are you afraid of?

The puppet's head comes back to life and looks at STEPHEN. ANNA and LUCY join MARK to operate the puppet.

Thoughts?

The puppet rises further.

Feelings?

The puppet rises further.

Actions?

With difficulty the puppet now stands and looks at STEPHEN.

MARK: And I looked at Lucy and I looked at Anna and then I looked at Dad. And just behind Dad's ear I saw... Dun Dun Da!

STEPHEN produces a red apple exactly like ANNA's.

Jupiter.

STEPHEN takes a bite out of the apple and holds it above his head.

And its big Red Spot.

Beat.

And that. That was the last thing.

Music changes. STEPHEN gently holds the apple like it was Jupiter. The puppet looks at Jupiter as the apple circles over-head, ending where it started. For the first time the whole stage, including the puppet, experience joy. Then the music changes and the puppet jumps into space. Very gently and very happily the puppet drifts off into space towards Jupiter and its big Red Spot.

Slowly fade to black.

End of play.